Introduction

Thank you for taking the time to download **Massage for Beginners**. This book will guide you through identifying and understanding the most common trigger points of your body. While you're learning the trigger points, the book will teach you effective self-massage techniques you can use with a tennis ball or with your bare hands.

This book also includes sections that will introduce you to some of the most popular self-massage tools available in the market today. It will also provide valuable tips on how you can apply massages on yourself, in consideration of trigger points and referred pain sites.

As essential as the other discussions in this book are the showcase of the benefits of massage, and a quick course on reflexology.

Once again, thanks for downloading this book, I hope you find it to be incredibly helpful!

Chapter 1: Understanding and Dealing with Trigger Points

When a muscle feels stiff and causes a certain degree of abnormal pain, it's normally classified as a trigger point by massage experts. For non-experts, this is just the tightness they feel in and around the muscle tissue. It is a knot that is the size of a pea or worse, a thumb.

This knot or the contracted muscle fiber can spread pain on nearby muscles, therefore causing another trigger point or a referred pain site. For example, a discomfort around your neck could spread around your shoulders and may even cause headaches. In this case, the trigger point should be in your neck because it is where the pain originated. Both your shoulders and your head are referred pain sites.

Knowing your trigger points allows you to work on one area, but address three concerns at the same time. Knowing how to massage yourself encourages you to apply a remedy immediately. Combining these knowledges certainly gives you an advantage over people who would rather hire someone to remedy the pain for them. Just imagine yourself not spending a single cent on expensive massage treatments and other forms of pain relievers.

Science and Differences

While there are still unanswered questions about the science and logic behind these trigger points, no one can deny the soothing effects of massaging them and their referred pain sites. For now, the only science you'd want to remember about trigger points is how they occur. Trigger points only occur in and around a muscle, or a group of muscles known as the myofascial trigger points. Pain originally occurring in a softer tissue of the skin, tendon, ligament or scar tissue is also a trigger point, but of a different kind.

In addition, a muscle tear, strain, or spasm cannot be considered myofascial trigger points. Remember that a muscle tear or a strain is a physical damage on the muscle or its tendons, while a spasm is an extreme contraction occurring in the entire muscle. A trigger point only occurs in a smaller portion of a specific muscle or a group of related muscles. Occasionally, a damaged muscle contributes to the occurrence of trigger points, but a spasm cannot become a trigger point or allow it to occur.

Pain Intervention

Some muscle pains could be a sign of more serious health problem, but interrupting the unwelcome sensation with a massage using your own hands, or tools like a tennis ball, should not make the problem any worse. The relief may sometimes be temporary, but stopping the pain cycle for a moment could at least help you think and perform, while waiting for an expert to diagnose and prescribe further treatment.

Beginner Tips in Applying Trigger Point Self-Massage

Addressing trigger points yourself, instead of hiring a massage therapist to relieve the pain, is a wise and practical way of perfecting the skill of self-massage. Below are some general tips you would want to keep in mind while learning self-massaging trigger points.

- Less to moderately painful knots may be fixed with light to moderate pressure with rubbings for only one or two days, while the toughest of trigger points may require the hardest of pressures, and may take six repetitions a day for a week before it heals.
- When dealing with a trigger point, hold and press on it for a minimum of ten seconds and a maximum of a minute-and-a-half. The strokes can be small circular or back-and forth, finger-pressing or palm-kneading motions.
- If you have an idea at what direction the muscle fibers of a specific muscle tissue go, you can apply strokes that are parallel to them muscle fibers. In this way, you are not just stretching the fibers, you are also making it easier to spot the trigger point. If you rub the muscle in a direction across its fibers, it is possible to mistake some spot as knots. Lastly, following the direction of the fibers with your strokes encourages oxygen and other nutrients to

flow freely in and out of the muscle you're working on.

- Remember to combine deep strokes and static pressure with your self-massages. Move the skin towards one direction with your fingers pressing on it. Hold the pressure on the trigger point for ten seconds. Only release the pressure at the end of the stroke and go back to repeat the steps.

- The amount of pressure you would be placing on the trigger point matters the most. This is because when you're massaging any part of your body, you are also sending signals to the nervous system. Therefore, always make sure to only feed it with a message it can tolerate. Otherwise, it will develop fear or trauma.

To work around this issue, use a scale that rates the level of pain a pressure brings. Scoring is from one to ten, with one as the softest and ten as the hardest pressure. In most cases though, you would want to apply pressure that is somewhere between four to seven in the scale.

- Always start with a level 1 pressure. This allows you to test the muscle's pain tolerance first. It also prevents you from shocking its receptors, as well as the nervous system. Increase the level once you're sure you can tolerate a harder pressure on a trigger point.

- When you're massaging yourself with your hands or any tool, the pressure on the knot should be strong enough, clear and satisfying. This is what massage experts call as "good pain". If you are wincing, gritting your teeth and cannot find yourself relaxing, you would want to adjust the pressure level a few notches down. If you don't, all your efforts of paining yourself would certainly all come to naught.

- As long as you're applying a reasonable amount of pressure on the trigger point, you are least likely to experience the massage session backfiring. If it is not causing any kind of immediate relief though, allow the trigger point to adapt to a higher pressure level within two to three days. On the contrary, if you cannot find yourself feeling comfortable even with softest pressure, the muscle is probably in a condition a self-massage could not fix.

Allow a therapist or a suitable doctor to check it and prescribe a different treatment on the trigger point.

- If you find yourself struggling to find the knot or the trigger point, manage your exploration by further dividing the muscle into sections. With a smaller section, it'll be easier to spot the knot or the bump. In some cases, you would just need to trust your instinct to determine the area where the pain is originating from. Again, it is not always the trigger point that causes the pain. At times, it is brought about by the referred pain site. Just think of a bullet that has been fired from a gun to shoot a target. The gun is the trigger point while the target is the referred pain site. Remember that your goal is to get rid of the gun.

- As soon as you've figured where the pain is originating from, massage it for as long as you want. Other experts recommend applying pressure on it for five minutes daily, but there is actually no time limit for addressing trigger points. As long as it is not causing you unreasonable and unbearable pain, continue massaging the trigger point until the pain is completely alleviated.

- After the massage, cover the massaged area with a hot pack wrapped in a damp towel or flannel. This will prevent harmful heat from touching your skin directly. The wrapping also absorbs and allows the massaged area to only receive relaxing warmth from the hot pack. Leave the hot pack on the massaged muscle for at least three minutes.

- As soon as the hot pack is removed, slowly and gently stretch the massaged area to its full range of movement thrice in a row. With each stretch, remember to take deep, relaxing breaths.

What you've learned so far are the general ways to handle a trigger point, while it's being massaged and after it's released. Some of these pointers may not apply to certain massage techniques, but it shouldn't stop you from trying to incorporate them with every self-massage you'll perform.

Chapter 2: Digging Deeper into Trigger Points and Pain Symptoms

The main benefit everyone gets from a massage is the release of pain-causing metabolites locked inside the muscle tissues of your body. The amount of extra money you have to spend on a massage therapy, the number of hours you can spare, and the quality of massage determine the number of physical pains you'd be saved from. But not any longer.

Learning self-massage gives you the freedom to control how much pain you can reduce and eliminate. Given this fact, it's just hard not to enumerate the different pains you'd soon say goodbye to. Some of these pains are mind-blogging, you thought only strong drugs could cure them.

Busting Pain Symptoms

Successfully releasing your trigger points relieve you from the following:

- Joint pains that are not actually caused by ligament injury, bursitis, tendonitis, and arthritis
- Symptoms similar to, but not caused by tennis elbow and carpal tunnel syndrome
- Lower and upper back pains
- Neck and jaw pains
- Headaches

The release of trigger points may also alleviate symptoms like:

- Difficulty of moving a certain body part at a normal range
- Unexplained weakness of a specific body part
- A tingling sensation on a specific muscle
- Numbness of a particular muscle
- A false pain in the heart
- Heartburn

- Dizziness and nausea
- Sinus congestion

The Reality of Learning Trigger Points

These symptoms are commonly experienced by people with unattended trigger points. Fortunately, you wouldn't need a trigger point manual to correctly pinpoint the origin of these pains. But what about the other symptoms or pains?

In reality, it'll take some time before you can be an expert with trigger points. However, knowing the different symptoms, and how a trigger point behaves in relation to a symptom should be enough for now.

To spot the trigger point without the manual, do not limit your search within the area where pain has manifested. Extend your search and include three more muscles nearby. Remember that a trigger point would typically refer pain to nearby muscles. If a certain area twitches and causes pain to shoot in muscles near it when pressed, then you've just spotted the trigger point.

What Causes Trigger Points?

There are many reasons why trigger points develop. Poor sleeping, standing and working positions develop trigger points. Excessive, repetitive and unusual body movements while exercising or doing any activity may cause them too. In some cases, the following health concerns cause trigger points:

- Abnormal processing of oxygen in the body caused by smoking, unhealthy sleeping patterns, inactivity, stress and tension
- Allergic reactions typically caused by yeast and dairy
- Hormonal imbalances caused by pre-menstrual and menopausal syndromes, hypothyroidism, and other hormonal conditions
- Yeast, viral and bacterial infections
- Vitamin and nutrient deficiencies especially in iron, vitamin B-Complex and vitamin C
- Strong medications

- Chronic internal illnesses
- Mechanical dysfunction or mechanical stresses like immobility, flat foot, short leg and poor posture
- Pressure on the nerve roots like sciatica

Acute symptoms are immediately after the application of treatment, while chronic pains may be eliminated in six weeks if you are persistent in applying a suitable massage technique.

Keeping Them at Bay

While massaging any trigger point or referred pain site does not always guarantee complete pain relief, there are ways to keep muscle discomfort at bay.

- Every muscle in your body deserves your conscious caring. Keep in mind that these are not designed to be held in fixed positions or contracted for a long period. As much as possible, vary your tasks daily. If you are supposed to complete almost the same tasks every day, find time to rest your overworked muscles.
- Apart from lifting things slowly, work at a reasonably slower pace, especially if an activity is deemed to cause muscle fatigue.
- Do passive stretches daily. It encourages your muscles to move at full range. Think of yourself as a cat who never fails to give its body a stretch after standing from rest or sleep.
- Spend time learning a specific relaxation activity like meditation and yoga.
- Observe and correct your posture whenever you are driving, when you're using your phone or computer, while you're reading or when you're sitting.
- Modify how a certain activity is completed. If you've been using the right hand to do a specific activity, practice using the left hand next time. In this case, you are not just encouraging balance, you are also developing a skill (ambidexterity).
- Always remember not to expose your muscles to extreme cold.

When you do, they contract and may inhibit flow of oxygen and other nutrients into it. When necessary, wear an extra piece of clothing like a sweater, or adjust the temperature of the heater.

- Strive to always eat a balance diet. Take vitamins and mineral supplements at least once a day, or as recommended by your physician.

There are 640 muscles in your body and it is possible for each muscle to be a trigger point or a referred pain site. As a beginner, you would only be focusing on the most common trigger points, although a comprehensive guide is available at triggerpoints.net. Until you get a reliable trigger points manual, you would have to deal with referred pain sites as indicated in the website provided. This would guide you through determining the trigger point given the actual site where the pain is occurring.

Chapter 3: Self -Massage Tools

Aside from your own hands, there are commercial massage tools you can use to combat those aching muscles in hard-to-reach areas of your body. These tools are not only reasonably-priced. Most of these tools are made of materials that can withstand even the toughest of pressures. Below are some of the most popular self-massage tools you can find in stores and online shops today.

1. Shiatsu Massage Belt

This versatile massage tool may be worn around the neck and the back. It uses infrared to emit heat, which helps tensed muscles to warm up. This results to a deep and relaxing electronic massage.

The belt also features a control that changes the direction of the massage from clockwise to counterclockwise.

To ensure it fits most sizes, the tool comes with a belt extension. The best of all, it is fully-automatic. The tool switches itself off. In case you fall asleep in the middle of a massage, no need to worry about overheating the device or wasting electrical energy.

Beurer MG148 is one of the most popular model and brand of the shiatsu massage belt.

2. Grid STK

This portable hand-held massager is made of durable foam that you simply roll across painful muscles until they're relieved of tension. The roller stick is also water resistant. You can use it while you are taking a warm bath.

Depending on how much force you would want applied on those sore leg muscles, the tool is available in two reasonable densities. So, if you are a runner or someone who frequently experiences muscle discomfort in and around the legs, the Grid STK is worth the purchase.

For maximum results, fitness experts recommend rolling the Grid STK across the muscles around the outside of your thighs before and after workout. This allows the muscles, especially the iliotibial band, to stretch, which reduces the risks of injury.

3. Twin Ball Massager by Oils of Life

Aside from being the most affordable, this self-massage tool is the easiest to carry around, as it is the smallest. The handle is similar to that of a shave, but instead of a blade, the opposite end is made of two small stainless steel balls.

If you want to re-energize the face, remove the puffiness around your eyes or both, you simply pull the twin balls across your face. The cooling effect and the rolling motion of the twin balls on your skin encourage blood circulation. As a result, skin elasticity is increased and wrinkles are reduced.

You can also use the twin ball massager on you palm to relieve it of its stress after spending hours cooking, typing, gardening, etc. Just roll the balls from the center of each palm to the lower joints of your fingers or the spaces between all of them.

Oils of Life Twin Ball Massager is available at The Body Shop.

4. Wellbeing Stress Spot Body Massager

Just like the twin ball massager, this is one of the cheapest yet most effective self-massage tools currently available in the market. It is rounded tool that features a wooden handle where you put your hand to grip on it. The handle has slots for your fingers to lock them in place. Across these wooden slots are rollers with rubber spikes.

This hand-held massager is best used on the thigh and upper arm muscles.

Hydrea /Fushi are the most common manufacturers of this product.

5. Spikey Massage Ball

If you want to immediately fix any after-workout pain, the spikey massage ball is your perfect solution. The rubber spikes can place sufficient and rewarding pressure on spots to quickly release trigger points. It is particularly recommended for gym goers who would like to target a number of muscle groups all at the same time.

While you are sitting on a chair or lying on the floor, place this ball under your back. Allow it to roll around the muscles on your back by moving your torso across the floor.

The Fitness Mad Spikey Massage Ball is available in two sizes – 7 and 9 centimeters.

6. Percussion Massager with Heat

This tool is one of the few compact massagers capable of providing deep tissue relaxation. It features two settings for speed and comes with four sets of spherical attachments that you can interchange depending on the amount of power you want your massage to have. The handle is also long enough so you can work on hard-to-reach areas such as your lower and upper backs.

This electronic device combines speed heat to provide a rewarding home spa experience and it is manufactured by Homemedics.

The product is currently available in Amazon.

7. Extreme Pro by GoFit

This roller is made of durable foam. This may seem typical for a massage roller, but this product by GoFit is designed like an egg crate to provide a self-massage experience you would want to do over and over. The design features hard rubber bumps that provide moderate to hard kneading action to release tension from your trigger points. It also features a hollow core to easily grip it.

The Extreme Pro may also double as an exercise tool. It is recommended as a complementary tool for people who perform core-strengthening exercises.

If you want to improve your posture and minimize the occurrence of trigger points, Extreme Pro is a practical choice of a corrector and a preventive tool rolled into one. Just position it below your spine for two minutes while you are lying on the floor. Experts also recommend using it on your hamstrings, quadriceps and calves to increase their flexibility.

8. Back Nodger

As what the name suggests, this self-massage tool was designed to replicate the effects of the walking stick cleverly used by elders to massage their backs. And it is effective!

The tool only has two parts- the head and the handle. The head is shaped like a club supported by a curved steel handle covered with a non-slip foam for easy grip. The curved design allows you to control the pressure you put on the head and then on the muscle.

The Back Nodger is sold at Boots.

Chapter 4: Tennis Ball Massage

Tennis ball has been mentioned several times in the previous chapters and you're probably wondering, why the tennis ball? What's in a tennis ball, anyway?

To summarize, the ball is made of two pieces of specialized rubber attached together to form the core. Once the core is formed, it is injected with pressurized gas, which provides most of the ball's bouncy quality. The shell is then covered with felt made of wool, nylon or a combination of both materials. Once the finishing touches are put in place, the tennis ball is packed and sent to the stores for selling.

Why a Tennis Ball?

In spite of the humble manufacturing process it undergoes, the tennis ball remains to be one of oldest, most effective and widely-used self-massage tool in the world, without the hassles of being costly, bulky, hard-t0-handle or bring. It is a primary massaging tool by choice because of three reasons – it rolls and it can withstand pressure.

Just imagine the force applied on a tennis ball from the time it is served in a game, up to the last time it is hit. A tennis ball boy may be required to replace it with a new one, but that does not mean it is damaged beyond use. Durability. That's the third reason.

Whether you are a dedicated gym goer or a hardworking office employee, massaging yourself with a tennis ball is a surefire way of releasing your trigger points and relieving you of any stress. Others may use golf balls or lacrosse balls, but a tennis ball is the recommended self-massage tool for beginners.

Basic Tennis Ball Massage

Unlike other massage therapies, a tennis ball massage can be applied on a daily basis without you worrying on adverse side effects. If you want to reduce or eliminate muscle sores and improve mobility at the shortest time possible, different tennis ball self- massage techniques can do the job for you. If you have a torn muscle or suspect you have one though, never apply any type of pressure on it, including that of a tennis ball's.

The general steps to applying a tennis ball massage on yourself are:

1. Determine where the trigger point is
2. Hold the ball's pressure on the affected muscle or trigger point for at least ten seconds
3. Release the pressure
4. Re-assess if you need to increase or reduce the amount of pressure you are putting on the muscle

5. Repeat step 2 as many times as possible
6. Find other trigger points by rolling the ball gently across the affected muscle area

Just like any massage, a tennis ball massage is guaranteed to cause pain. Remember that the pain may increase upon locating the actual trigger point with the ball. But as you hold the pressure against the muscle, it should diminish gradually. Otherwise, you might need to forego the massage session and have the muscle checked by a medical expert for any damage or injury.

Upper Body Tennis Ball Massages

The Deltoids

The entire area of your shoulders is covered by a muscle known as the deltoid. It is one of the upper body muscles that experience frequent tightness and weakness. At times, you do not have a choice but to limit its movement because of the extreme pain you feel in an around the fibers found in the muscle's anterior (section near the chest), lateral (next to the anterior) and the posterior (closest to the shoulder blade).

If you want to hit all of these sections right and ease the pain that you are feeling, you can use two effective tennis ball massage techniques.

Massage #1

The first technique requires you to stand on your side against a sturdy wall. At this position, carefully place the ball on your upper arm. Press the ball on the wall with your upper arm while you move it from side to side or up and down. This method is recommended in remedying mild to moderate shoulder pains.

Massage #2

If the pain is between moderate to extreme but bearable, and you think you can tolerate a harder pressure on your shoulder, this second position is highly-recommended. First, you need to lie on the floor on your side. Place the tennis ball between your shoulders and the flat surface. Roll the ball from left to right or up and down with your shoulders. As you are rolling, limit the range of your movement so you would not displace the ball.

Since all of your weight is pushed against the ball and the opposing force from the ball and the ground is as strong, the pressure you would feel on your deltoid is stronger in this position than in the standing position. Just remember, if neither of the positions are giving you the satisfaction nor the relief, you might be dealing with a more serious muscle condition, which may require a doctor's intervention.

The Scapula

Latisimuss Dorsi or your lats are directly attached to each of your shoulder blades or scapula. If you try to reach your shoulder blade with your hand, your lats is where the top of your hand would initially rest before it reaches the blade. If you have reached for you shoulder blade and felt a little sore around the lats area, it is definitely time to give it some tennis ball massage.

Massage #1

With your back against the wall, put the ball on your back just below your shoulder blade. Hold the ball in position as you press it against the wall. Maintain or increase the pressure by pushing your back harder on the wall as you base your left-and-right movement on the curvature of your shoulder blades.

Massage #2

With your back against the floor, place the ball underneath your armpits and move to your side. Make sure the side where the ball is placed is directly facing the floor. As soon as you are in this position, carefully stretch the arm of this side outwards. You know you have successfully positioned yourself once you feel the ball move slightly below the outer part of your shoulder blade. At this point, slightly roll the ball in your preferred direction with the pressure coming from your weight.

Never ignore any soreness around your lats. In most cases, pain in this area could cause or has already triggered a shoulder imbalance.

The Rotator Cuffs

As the name suggests, rotator cuffs are muscles and tendons that enables your shoulder to rotate. Your rotator cuff muscles are further classified as the infraspinatus and the teres minor. These muscles become exhausted when you frequently stretch your arms over your shoulder and your head.

If you always do things that require extending your arms over your head, you might want to apply some tennis ball pressure around your rotator cuffs to relieve it from stiffness and to allow it to move at full range.

Massage #1

Similar to massaging your lats with the ball, lay on your side for on the floor. This time, position your elbow on this side at a ninety-degree angle while the ball is under this side's rotator cuff muscle. The angle on your elbow allows the muscle to slightly protrude and secure the ball in its position. With your body weight pushing against the ball, roll the ball in small rotating or up-and-down fashion with your upper back.

Massage#2

You can also do this by standing with your back against the wall. Just place the ball just outside your shoulder blade. Remember, this can turn into the most painful yet most satisfying tennis ball massage you can ever apply on your upper back!

The Trapezius Muscle

The trapezius muscle is found on either side of your upper back. It is shaped like a triangle, which allows the head to extend at the neck. It also balances the shoulder blades, rotates them and moves them, too.

Since these parts of the upper body are always used in a lot of activities, including when you are sleeping, it will be a good idea to frequently release pressure locked up within their partner muscles.

Recommended Massage Technique

While you can apply a ball massage on these muscles while standing, most experts recommend doing it while lying on the floor. Simply place the ball on top of the obvious bulge on the side of your neck and then lie on your back. To apply more pressure, bend your knees up to a certain degree. The more you bend your knees, the bigger your angular movements and the stronger the pressure on the muscles can become.

The Pectoralis Muscles

Unlike what most people think, prolonged sitting can also cause tightness around your chest muscles known as the pectoralis major and pectoralis minor. The tightness occurs internally and might cause pain and other issues on your shoulders, if not addressed as soon as possible.

Facing the Wall and the Floor Massage

To eliminate the soreness around your pecs, follow the same steps in administering a ball massage on the other upper body muscles. The only difference is you would be facing the wall or the floor this time since the ball would be perched just below the chest. As soon as you feel the ball's pressure on your chest, begin rolling the ball around the muscle to locate the trigger point. In most cases, the trigger point is found nearest your shoulder. This is known as the pectorial insertion. It is also the muscle area just below your collar bone.

Similar to other tennis ball massage techniques, doing this against the floor can yield more pressure than applying it using a vertical surface.

The Levator Scapula

The levator scapula is a muscle connecting your shoulder blade to your cervical spine. This is why maintaining a good posture helps prevent developing soreness around this muscle. Otherwise, you would need to correct your posture and perform a ball massage on it.

Recommended Massage Technique

Since this involves your posture, you'd be applying the massage in a standing position. To begin, place the ball just on top of your shoulder blade. This spot is also the area located directly below the back and sides of your neck.

Once you feel the pressure from the ball on your levator scapula, make small clockwise or counterclockwise movements using your shoulders. If you would raise the connecting arm while massaging the muscle, the pressure is maximized, making it easier to spot the trigger point.

The Hands and the Wrists

Routine hand movements often cause pain. If left unattended, the pain may become more violent and can turn into a carpal tunnel syndrome. This syndrome occurs when the median nerve found in your hand swells and affects the performance of the surrounding tendons, tendon sheaths and ligaments. Furthermore, this syndrome results to the obstruction of the actual carpal tunnel where sensation from the median nerve passes through to affect the movement of the thumb, the index, middle and ring fingers.

If you constantly engage in tasks that require moving your wrists, hands and fingers over a long period, resting and applying a ball massage on them could help correct symptoms or even cure the syndrome.

Below are four ways of applying a tennis ball massage on your hands:

1. Finger Stretching

Place the ball on a flat surface. While sitting or standing, put one finger on top of the ball with your palm facing the surface. Slowly force the finger on the ball as you push the hand downwards. Remember to hold this position for at least ten seconds. You can also slide the finger off the ball and towards you to maximize the effects. Repeat the steps with the same finger and the other fingers as desired.

2. Wrist Massage

Hold the ball with one hand and directly place it on the other wrist. Press and move the ball slowly and in circular motion across the tendons of your wrist. As soon as you feel the hand and fingers relax, move the ball to the other hand and repeat the same steps.

3. Rolling Massage

Similar to the finger stretching technique, place the ball on a flat surface and place your hand over it. Open your palm and press the ball with it. Once you feel the pressure on your palm, begin rolling it in circular or up-and-down motion. As soon as the tightness is released, switch hands and repeat the previous steps.

4. Squeeze Massage

You simply grab the ball with one hand like you are trying to hide it entirely from sight. As soon as you have a firm grasp on the ball, squeeze it as tightly as you can. Hold your squeeze for at least five seconds and release it. You can repeat the steps as desired and then switch hands with after two or three repetitions.

Lower Body Tennis Ball Massages

The ITB

Whether you are physically active or not, there are instances where you would experience unexplainable discomfort in and around your iliotibial band. The iliotibial band or ITB is a ligament that runs lengthwise from the sides of your knees, up to your thighs, and then at the top of your hips.

The ITB is responsible for stabilizing both your hips and knees when you are running or brisk walking. When these ligaments become thick and rub on your bones, they swell and cause pain.

While beginners are advised to massage pain or tightness away from these ligaments using foam rollers first, you can move on to using a tennis ball if you feel you can tolerate the pressure and pain the ball may place on it.

Recommended Massage Technique

To administer the massage, place the ball on the floor and lay sideways on it. Make sure the ball is directly under the sides of your knees. In this position, roll the ball slowly and gently all the way to your hip. This means you'll have to move your body downwards. While the ball is moving upwards, try feeling the pressure. Calculate whether you would need to apply more force on the ball or decrease it depending on your pain tolerance. In addition, focus more on the upper portion of your ITB as this is where most of the trigger points are located.

The TFL

The tensor fasciae latae or TFL is a muscle found between the ITB and your hip bone. It provides side-to-side knee stability. It also allows the hip to flex and abduct when you are walking or keeping a foot ahead of the other. If you love skiing or horseback riding, you use this muscle frequently. Prolonged sitting may cause it to shorten and bring about a tight feeling around it.

Recommended Massage Technique

If you experience pain in this muscle, lay on the floor with the TFL section over the tennis ball. Roll the ball around the area until you spot the trigger point. Hold the pressure against the trigger point for at least ten seconds and then release.

The Calves

Your calves comprise the soleus and the gastrocnemius muscles where a lot of trigger points appear. Prolonged standing, continuous running and walking may cause pain in and around your calves.

Recommended Massage Technique

You can apply tennis ball massage on your calves while lying on the floor. However, considering the calves' width and the difficulty of administering a massage while most of your body is resting flat on the floor, beginners are recommended to apply this technique while sitting.

Grasp the ball with one hand. Make sure your feet are flat on the floor and knees are bent to form a ninety-degree angle on each side. Extend your hand on one calf and force the ball against it. Roll it up and down or in circular motion to locate the trigger point. Once you have determined the trigger point, hold the pressure at the spot for at least ten seconds or as desired. Repeat the same steps with the other calf.

The Buttocks

Mainly responsible for moving and protecting your hips and thighs are your gluteus muscles - the gluteus minimus, gluteus medius and gluteus maximus. These muscles are just three of the strongest muscles in your body and are found in your buttocks. If you feel tight or sore around this area, at least one of your gluteus muscles needs some tension release.

Massage #1

To release tension from any or all of your buttocks' muscles, lay on your side with the ball just on one side of your buttocks. This is the section that is located slightly further at the back of your TFL. You're focusing on this section because it is actually your gluteus maximus where most trigger points are found.

As soon as you've positioned the ball at the correct starting point, roll on your buttocks and move the ball around until you find the trigger point. Force your weight against the ball with your hips, hold it just under the trigger point for at least ten seconds, and then release. Repeat as desired or until the tightness has completely diminished.

Massage #2

You can also massage your buttocks with the ball while sitting on the ground. While your hands are resting on your sides against the floor, and your legs are bent, place the ball under the left side of your buttocks. At this point, lift your left foot, straighten your leg and start pulling and pushing your body to roll the ball under your buttocks. Stop and push your weight on the ball for at least ten seconds when you come across a tight spot. Repeat as desired and follow the same steps for the other side of the buttocks.

The Piriformis Muscle

It may be small, but the piriformis muscle is a big help in terms of rotating your hips. Located between your thighbone and lower spine, just beneath your buttocks or gluteus maximus muscle, the piriformis muscle also aids the lower body in turning your legs and feet outwards.

Recommended Massage

To relieve pain in this muscle, sit on the ball and roll it around your buttocks. Once you figure where the trigger point is, stretch your legs to lessen the pain the pressure could send down to your leg muscles. Apply the force for at least ten seconds or for as long as you can tolerate the pain. The reason behind the shooting pain is the sciatic nerve connecting the piriformis muscle to your thigh and leg muscles. Repeat rolling the ball several times or as necessary.

The Legs

Peroneals are muscles located around each leg. They also receive and store tension, causing tightness and pain in other lower body parts, especially in the knees.

Massage #1

To eliminate tension within your peroneals, apply tennis ball massage around each leg while you're sitting on the floor. Place the ball on the floor and put the outer side of your leg above it. Move your leg up and down to roll the ball underneath, while pushing your leg's weight on it for added pressure. Slowly rotate your leg with each full stroke to make sure you also cover the back part and the inner side. Repeat these steps with the other leg.

Massage #2

You can also roll the ball around your leg muscles with the ball cupped in your palm. Just remember to always hold the pressure on each trigger point for at least ten seconds on both techniques.

The Feet

Just because there is hardly any trigger point in your feet, they don't need to be massaged. Your feet are still one of the most overworked parts of your entire body. Therefore, they need to be pampered every so often. Besides, applying some pressure on them could loosen fascia and improve their mobility.

Recommended Massage

Place your foot on top of the ball. Roll it from the ball, then to the heel and back. Since you are not locating any trigger point, just hold the pressure on an area where you mostly feel the pain or tightness. It can be the center, the ball or the heel. Use the same steps with the other foot and repeat as needed.

In case you're wondering, this foot massage technique could be done sitting or standing. If you want to increase the pressure though, you might want to push all of your weight down on the ball by standing up.

Relieving Tension Headaches

Tension headaches sometimes emanate from the back of your head. Since the trapezius is the typical trigger point for headaches, following the steps in massaging your neck should be enough to alleviate the pain. If a trapezius muscle massage fails to complete the job, applying a tennis ball rub on the back of your head might just do the trick.

First, lie on your back and place a ball in the space between your forefinger and thumb. Since you'd be using your hands at the same time with this technique, you'd be needing two tennis balls.

Once a ball is placed on either hand, place them at the back of your neck. You'd know you've positioned your hands with the balls correctly as soon as you feel both balls nudging the left and right side of your skull's base. Rest your head on the balls while making sure you don't lose holding them in place.

From this position, slowly turn your head to your right. While doing so, determine at what point the pain suddenly shoots up. This is where you'd want to hold the pressure on your next repetition. Go back to the starting position and then turn to opposite direction. Complete as many repetitions as needed.

You may also tuck and lift your chin using the same pace to complement with the left-to-right movement of this technique.

To easily and quickly determine which muscle to target (trigger point) when you feel a certain pain in a specific body part (referred pain site), you may refer to the table below.

Pain Location and Target Muscle Cheat Sheet

Pain Location	Target Muscle
Head	Trapezius
Neck	Trapezius
Shoulders	Scapula, Rotator Cuffs, Pecs, Deltoids and Trapezius
Back	Hip Rotators, TFL and Glutes
Hip	Hip Rotators, TFL and Glutes
Chest	Deltoids and Pecs
Knee	Calves, TFL, Glutes and Quads

As a beginner, it is best to regularly apply tennis ball massage on each of the muscles or body parts discussed in this chapter. Just keep in mind that more than the rubbing, the pressure applied on each trigger point is the most important.

Chapter 4: Quick Anti-Stress Massages

Working from eight to five, for five consecutive days, could bring a great deal of stress. Most of the time, this is manifested as a symptom or a combination of symptoms like a headache combined with muscle pain in different parts of the body. Unfortunately, a lot of people still tend to ignore stress and its symptoms until the other aspects of their lives are negatively affected.

Never ignore stress, especially symptoms that can affect your work productivity and performance. Neglect of your well-being could easily cost the promotion you've long been waiting for. So, how do you address stress and its symptoms, considering you only have two days a week for yourself? What if your time off from work is not enough to even complete eight hours of sleep?

The truth is you cannot address all manifestations of stress at the same time. But there is at least one major symptom you can fix on a regular basis. These are the tension the different muscles in your body have accumulated over time. Instead of using your idle time just to browse the net, chat with your colleagues or even smoke, why not give yourself a real and quick stress-relief? Whenever and wherever, you can use your hands to release unwanted tension from your body. If you think about it, self-massage techniques done regularly are great habits that could change your lifestyle for the better and improve your health and well-being.

Dealing with Headaches

Working in front of the computer is commonly the cause of tension headache. Instead of taking a pain reliever drug, spend a few minutes of your lunch break or coffee break to relieve the headache.

You'll need to use both hands in this massage technique (one hand for each side of the face). First, place your thumbs on the part of your cheekbones nearest to your ears for support. Then with your index fingers, slowly apply pressure on your temples. At this point, consider how much pressure you'd like to put on them. Once you're decided with the pressure, rub the temples in a circular motion while maintaining the pressure you like.

After at least sixty seconds, gently move your fingers across your hairline until fingers of both hands meet around the middle of your forehead. Massage your forehead and entire scalp with small and quick finger tapping movements. To help you with the movement, just imagine how tiny raindrops fall on your head. Repeat all steps as needed.

Pampering Your Hands and Fingers

Along with headaches come tired hands and fingers. While computer users are often reminded to give their hands a rest after at least an hour of continuous typing, most of them forget to do so. To ensure you won't forget, set your computer alarm to remind you during your entire shift to relax your hands every hour.

When the alarm sets off, begin stretching your hands and fingers. Using one hand, massage each finger of the other hand by twisting and pulling as you go from the base to the tip. Repeat the steps for each finger or as needed. Just remember to switch hands afterwards.

After massaging all fingers of both hands, place one hand upwards on your lap or on your desk. With the other hand's thumb. squeeze the fleshy part of the palm in between your thumb and index finger. Rub this area in an upwards motion while placing a reasonable amount of pressure on it. From this area, move on to the other sections of your palm using the same rubbing technique. To help you rub on the correct spot, just imagine a line running from the middle of your wrist to the web-like section in between your index and middle fingers, ring and middle fingers, and the baby and ring fingers.

You can also follow the above steps in massaging the sides of your palm. These are the sections on the side of your baby finger down to the side nearest the small protruding bone at the back of your wrist; and the area on the side of your thumb down to the side of its fleshy base near the wrist.

Apart from relieving your hands of stress, massaging the different sections can reduce or eliminate pain from the other parts of the body. It can also contribute to the complete treatment of certain diseases. As you may already know, a lot of experts use hand reflexology charts to help them address certain health conditions by massaging specific sections of the hands.

Releasing Neck Tension

The neck is one of the most sensitive parts of the body. Most people would rather hire masseurs to release the tension locked within their neck muscles than do it themselves. You might follow suit but don't! There is an easy way to massage your neck without worrying you'd aggravate the pain or injure it.

You'd want to begin by sitting in front of your desk. Put your hands together by interlocking your fingers and placing them at the back your neck. Slightly drop your head forward and start massaging your neck with your thumbs. While applying moderate pressure, rub the muscles on your neck as your glide your thumbs upwards. You can stop and repeat the steps once your thumbs reach past the base of your head.

With your fingers still locked together at the back of your neck, stretch your neck muscles and your spine by gently pushing your head towards your desk with your hands. Follow the direction of the pressure by slightly dropping your head forward as soon as you feel your hands pushing the back of your neck.

Move one hand across your chest to rest it on the opposite shoulder. With the tip of your fingers, apply moderate pressure on the flesh surrounding your shoulder as you slowly move towards your neck and then finishing at the base of your head near your ears. Repeat the same steps with the other side of the shoulder and neck.

Working Your Stressed Lower Back

A lot of employees take a leave from work because of severe lower back pain. If they only knew how to stop it from getting any worse, they could have saved that day for other important matters. Fortunately, you don't have to be like them now that you'd learn a simple lower back massage technique.

While you're standing, place your hands around your waist. Make sure your thumbs are behind and the rest of your fingers are in front. In this position, press on the flesh where your thumbs are resting. Determine how much pressure both sides need and adjust it based on your tolerance for pain. Sustain the pressure you want as you rub your lower back with your thumbs using gentle circular motions.

Move your thumbs as far as they can go on your lower back and apply the same massaging technique in those areas. Just remember not to press directly on your spine.

You can also change the direction of your movement from going inwards to moving downwards to your sacrum's bony surface. Maintain rubbing and gliding an inch at a time to spot tender areas. Whenever a thumb runs into tender spot, make sure to stop, add more thumb pressure on that area, and hold it there for at least ten seconds before your release and move on.

Another rewarding lower back massage technique is placing your palms on the muscles just above your waist and opposite your tummy. Your fingers should be facing downwards when you start kneading the base of your palm and pressing with your fingers. The trick to successfully applying this technique is to imagine grabbing these muscles off your back.

Relaxing the Feet

Your feet might be resting on the floor for the rest of the day, but it's never safe from accumulating stress. Why?

Your body weight is forced towards your feet. Even if you're seated, you are still forcing it down to your feet and not on the floor. This is to balance yourself as you lean towards and away from your desk.

Massaging your feet at your desk in the presence of other people is absolutely disrespectful and unprofessional. If you really need to relieve your feet of its burden, excuse yourself and find a vacant room or a cubicle in the washroom.

As soon as you are seated, remove your shoes and place your foot at top of the opposite knee. Using the thumb of the opposite hand (left foot is to right hand, and right foot is to left hand), press the sides of the foot firmly. Work your thumb from the heel up to the side of the big toe's base.

At this point, slowly move your thumb towards the smallest toe while pressing on the ridges just at base of the toes. The ridges are the spaces where the bones of your toes are separated.

Upon reaching the base of the smallest toe, move your thumb and index finger at its tip. Gently twist and squeeze the toe as you work your way down to its base with these fingers. Repeat these steps with the other toes.

When you're done twisting and squeezing the last toe, grab all five toes with your hand. Push and pull the toes with your hand to give them a much-needed stretch.

While the hand on the same side is supporting the top of the foot you're massaging, form a fist with the opposite hand and gently force your knuckles at the bottom of the foot you're working on. While sustaining the pressure of your knuckles on the foot, you should work your way from the heel to the ball with small rotating movements. Rub your way back to the heel using the same movement.

As soon as you've completed several repetitions, flex the toes of the foot you just massaged. Extend the foot and rotate the ankle several times. Rest it on the floor for a minute before you start working on the other foot using same steps.

Massaging Your Jaw

When you're nervous or stressed, your jaw would sometimes feel sore. At times, it would feel like it's going to lock as soon as you attempt to open your mouth. Before this actually happens, relax your jaw with a simple massage using only your fingers.

With your fingertips, slowly push the skin of your jaw's baseline towards your cheeks and then to your cheekbones. As you find your fingers sliding up to your cheeks, open your mouth and then close it as soon as your fingers reach your cheekbones. Gently slide those fingers back to its starting position. If you're not doing this in front of the mirror, imagining a beard line would make it easier to repeat the steps as needed.

Another way to relax your jaw is to place your fingers directly on the jaw bone located just below your sideburns and parallel to the tips of your earlobes. Remember that you'd be using both hands in this massage technique (one hand for each side of the face). As soon as each set of fingers is placed at the right spot on each side of your face, gently press both areas and make small rotating rubs with your fingertips. While you're rubbing these spots, open and close your mouth like you did in previous technique.

After about a minute, move your fingers down to your chin. Place your thumbs under the chin and your fingers on your lower jaw. With your fingertips just below your lower lip, pull the skin down to your chin repeatedly. Remember to apply some pressure each time your fingertips are back at the starting position.

Unknotting Knee Tension

Prolonged sitting may transfer some unbearable pain to your knees. If they're bended for too long, they tend to bind connective tissues.

To unknot these tissues, straighten your legs while you're seated and allow your heels to rest on the floor. Hold this position for at least a minute to relax your quads, which are the muscles located in front of your thighs.

In the same position, start massaging your quads with your knuckles or fingertips for ten seconds. Massage your quads as if you're drawing a star with your fingers or knuckles. After this, bend and unbend your legs twice. You can repeat all of the steps as needed, focusing on applying more pressure on areas that are tensed and painful.

Again, these are quick self-massage fixes. Remember not to overdo these techniques though. If you don't feel any improvement or the pain worsens, discontinue massaging yourself and immediately visit your clinic for proper diagnosis and treatment.

Chapter 5: Basic Reflexology

Although it follows a different principle and only uses a limited number of techniques, reflexology offers health benefits you surely wouldn't want to pass on.

Here are some of its known benefits:

- *It improves blood circulation.*

When this occurs, it is easier for oxygen to pass through vital organs, therefore optimizing their functions. Oxygen also promotes cellular repair and growth.

- *It helps eliminate toxins from the body.*

Because of its known ability to clear the urinary tract and to improve bladder functions, reflexology should be given credit for the elimination of unhealthy substances in the body.

- *It stimulates the brain.*

Reflexology opens your neural pathways allowing oxygen and energy to pass to reach the different parts of your nervous system, specifically your brain. This is why people's moods are boosted after a reflexology session. In addition, reflexology can improve your memory and other cognitive skills.

- *It relaxes the body and the mind.*

Since it follows the same principle of releasing stress through pressing, it has a strong ability of putting both your mind and body in a rested stated.

Life Force Principle

The main principle of reflexology is to squeeze on pressure points to allow energy or "life force" to pass through the body and heal illnesses, strains and injuries. Like any other type of massage, it focuses on pressure points. Although this time, the pressure points are located in just three parts of the body- the hands, the feet and the ears.

Since the focus is limited to only these parts, you don't need to remove your clothes when administering self-reflexology. It also wouldn't require the use of tools, lotions or oils. All you need are your fingers and a sufficient knowledge of the reflexology chart. You can find the charts in this website- handreflexologycharts.com

Common Hand Reflex Points

As a beginner, you'll focus on reflex points found in your hands. You're concentrating on your hands not just because it's fully accessible, but also because you can administer self-reflexology on your hands anytime and anywhere.

Reflex points are pressure points that you manipulate with your fingers to affect a certain body part or organ. You can locate several reflex points on your palm, as well as the back and the top of your hand. Just keep in mind that all reflex points on one hand mirror the reflex points on the other.

The following are some reflexology techniques you can use to alleviate common health problems:

- *Digestive problems*

    The corresponding reflex point for your intestines and other digestive organs is the base of your palms. You can manipulate this area using the tip of your fingers or knuckles.

    1. Form as fist with one hand.
    2. Place the other hand over the fist.
    3. Move either hand so the base of the palm is directly touching the knuckles of the other hand.
    4. Roll the heel of your palm over the knuckles or the knuckles on the other heel of your palm.
    5. For added pressure, move both hands in the same direction for at least a minute. Doing this at least twice a week will improve your

digestive functions.

- *Insomnia and Sleep Disorders*

In reflexology, the middle of your thumb is connected to your pituitary gland, the part of the brain responsible for regulating and controlling sleep. If you want your slept to be restful or beat insomnia, massaging your thumb could help.

1. Locate the middle of your thumb print.
2. With the side of the opposite thumb's nail, press this part and hold for at least forty-five seconds.
3. Since both thumbs should affect the same part of the brain, you can apply the pressure on the other thumb as needed. Reflexologist recommended performing the massage a maximum of three times per day.

- *Flu and colds*

When you have a cold or you're down with a flu, your sinuses are clogged and may cause you headaches. Your clue that your sinuses are congested would be your fingers feeling puffy and tight. This is because they're the reflex points for your sinuses.

To unblock the sinuses, try massaging your fingers at least four times a day.

1. Using the other hand's thumb and index finger, press and rub all fingers from base to the tip.
2. For optimal effect, stop at each joint and press harder. Hold the pressure for at least five seconds. Experts recommend performing this technique on all fingers at least four times a day.

- *Back Pains*

If your back is sore, notice that the side of your hand would feel a bit tender as well, especially the spot from the side of your wrist up to the side of your thumb. Apart from the quick massages you can apply on your back, working on the corresponding reflex points will help you relieve the pain the soonest possible time.

1. Hold both palms up.
2. Place one hand on top of the other palm.
3. The base of the top hand's fingers should rest in the space between the bottom hand's thumb and index fingers. Fold your fingers to touch the back of the bottom hand.
4. Using the top hand's thumb, rub the entire length of the bottom hand's sides with moderate to hard pressure.
5. Allow your thumb to hold the pressure on the fleshy part of the other hand for at least fifteen seconds. Switch hands after several repetitions.
6. Perform this reflex point massage four times a day.

Reflexology and its health benefits may not be as widely accepted as the massages and their benefits, but it has proven itself many times for the past hundreds of years. While the world has yet to prove the science behind the claims of this traditional therapy, it is considered one of the safest ways to remedy pains and illnesses. As long as you remain reasonable in dealing with your pains and ailments, there is absolutely nothing wrong with incorporating reflexology with doctor-prescribed treatments.

Conclusion

Thanks again for taking the time to download this book!

I hope that from this point on, you will use what you've learned from this book when dealing with muscle pains.

I hope that the practical self-massage techniques taught in this book will help you lead a stress-free life.

Please feel free to share the knowledge you just gained with the people closest to your heart. As they say, there is nothing more fulfilling than knowing your loved ones could follow your lead towards a better well-being.

If you enjoyed this book, please take the time to leave me a review on Amazon. I appreciate your honest feedback, and it really helps me to continue producing high quality books.

Simply CLICK HERE to leave a review, or click on the link: https://www.amazon.co.uk/Massage-Beginners-Guide-Trigger-Points-ebook/dp/B01J5AHVPW.

Printed in Great Britain
by Amazon